A Pilgrim's Path:

31 Days to Discovering Life IN Christ

By

Brad Riley

Ashley,
May these words be a
blessing on your journey!
Thanks for being a Pilgrim
on the Path with me!

Shalom

Brad Riley

ISBN-13 978-1539407799

Printed in the United States of America

Cover Design: Brad Riley

Cover Photo: Garden of Gethsemane by Brad Riley 2011

Dedicated to...

Pastor Gene Williams, of Blessed Memory, and his wife Joyce who mentored me in my faith for over 30 years. My love for the Bible was greatly enhanced by Pastor Gene's challenging and meaningful sermons, and my dream to visit the Holy Land was realized on my first pilgrimage with them. This book would not have been possible without Joyce's support for and encouragement of my writing.

Also

To Ron and Renae Ryan whose support for me, my family, and my ministry have been invaluable.

Table of Contents

Introduction

In America, when we hear the word pilgrim, we usually think of tall black hats, turkeys and Thanksgiving. Rarely do we think of ourselves. Yet each of us is a pilgrim, whether we realize it or not. We're all on a journey to somewhere. A pilgrim, by definition, is a person on a journey, but not just any journey to anywhere. A pilgrim's journey is a journey toward something of significance.

Sadly, there are people in the world who seem to wander through each day as if they are going nowhere. Life, it seems is always the enemy. Things seem to go wrong a lot more than they go right. As they drift through life, they rarely learn from their experiences. They try to get by just one more day, hoping things will be better tomorrow, often wondering, what's the point to all of it.

To live a life of significance, we must begin with the understanding that not only does life matter. We matter. The ultimate significance of life is found when we understand that we matter to God. We matter to God not because of anything we have done, but simply because we exist. Human beings are the crown jewel in all God's creation, and it grieves Him to see His children living below the blessing we deserve.

Ever since the fall of Adam and Eve in the Garden, humanity has been on a pilgrimage... a search for significance. Our journey, once we begin to pay attention, causes us to delve deeply into ourselves and the world around us, searching for answers to the first order questions of life: Who am I? Why am I here? How should I live?

In 2011, I was blessed to go on a pilgrimage to Israel with Foundations of Faith. I can't tell you how meaningful that trip was. The time to contemplate my faith in the very place where Jesus lived was priceless: I walked where Jesus walked, sailed across the Sea of Galilee, felt the striated pavement where Jesus' flesh was ripped from His back, and then looked into the empty tomb. My faith was enriched beyond measure. I felt Christ living deep within me.

This book was written to help pilgrims on a journey, whether at home or on a trip to the Holy Land. We don't have to re-invent the wheel in trying to find all the answers we seek. There is a life that revealed all the answers to all the questions of life, and there is a record of that life from which, everyone can find the answers. That life was Jesus of Nazareth. The record is His gospel.

In this book you will find a 31-day devotional pilgrimage that invites you to walk through some of the events of Jesus' life as recorded in His gospels. The significance for which we all seek is not only to be found "in Christ", for all who believe are said to be "in Him". But rather, as believers we must also seek to discover what it means to "live 'IN' Christ". It is "in" Christ that St. Paul says we can live as "new creatures" (2 Cor.5:17).

I hope this book will help you face some of the many pitfalls that accompany all who dare to go on a pilgrimage of such significance. I pray you will discover how to face your fears, make right choices in a wrong world, find true Sabbath rest, and many more things that our Lord Jesus wants to show you on your journey.

It is also my prayer that your time in this book will be accompanied by prayer and reflection of not only the devotional thoughts shared, but most significantly, of the passages of scripture on which they are based. There simply is no substitute for time to reflect on and commune intimately with our most Holy God – Father, Son and Holy Spirit, and the depth of His word.

Consider these thoughts from the late Brennan Manning as you begin your pilgrimage:

*"The Word we study has to be the Word we pray. My personal experience of the relentless tenderness of God came not from exegetes, theologians, and spiritual writers, but from sitting still in the presence of the living Word and beseeching Him to help me understand with my head and heart His written Word. Sheer scholarship alone cannot reveal to us the gospel of grace. We must never allow the authority of books, institutions, or leaders to replace the authority of *knowing* Jesus Christ personally and directly."*

- Brennan Manning, The Ragamuffin Gospel: Good News for the Bedraggled, Beat-up, and Burnt Out

And so my fellow Pilgrims, let us set out together on the path to Life IN Christ. In the words of Jesus to His disciples, "Rise, let us be going;" (Mark 14:42)

-Brad Riley

Day 1

Don't Wait for Victory

As it is written in the book of the words of Isaiah the prophet, "The voice of one crying in the wilderness: Prepare the way of the Lord, make his paths straight. Every valley shall be filled, and every mountain and hill shall be brought low, and the crooked shall be made straight, and the rough ways shall be made smooth; and all flesh shall see the salvation of God."

Mark 1:4-6

When we read the words of Isaiah that John proclaimed, we often concentrate on a futuristic interpretation. We hear things like, every mountain being made low and valleys being filled and we say, "That must be in the Second Advent of Jesus because our lives still have a lot of ups and downs in the here and now." It seems our lives are anything but the smooth and straight as Isaiah prophesied. But today, let's hear this prophecy with new ears. Let's do as Isaiah says and, "prepare the way of the Lord". When we open the way for Jesus to live and move in our lives we find victory.

All the things Isaiah prophesied will be true in the Second Advent of Jesus. But, if we open our hearts to the life in Christ the New Testament offers, we will have all these victories now. We don't have to wait to live such lives. We don't have to wait for victory.

Life in Christ is about living by faith so the mountains in our lives can be overcome, and the valleys can be filled up with meaning and understanding, all by the grace and mercy of our Lord Jesus. We don't have to live down and out. While life may seem like a long and winding road, when we trust in Christ with all our heart and don't lean on our own understanding (Proverbs 3:5, 6), He will direct our path. These are the victories of life in Christ.

Our job is to live as Isaiah prophesied. We are to prepare the way of the Lord in our lives so that He can make the rough way smooth. Isaiah didn't say Jesus would take the rough path away, but that he would make it smooth. Jesus makes the ups and downs of this life bearable by the grace of His Holy Spirit living in us...This is victory...This is life in Christ.

Notes

Discoveries from my path...

Day 2

"I have said this to you in figures; the hour is coming when I shall no longer speak to you in figures but tell you plainly of the Father."

John 16:25

Friends with Benefits

While I'm sure it wasn't New Year's Eve on the night before Jesus died, it certainly was a new beginning for the Disciples. Jesus was promoting them from student followers, to friends with benefits; benefits that would fill them with great joy. As a disciple of Jesus, we too are his friends.

Until that night, Jesus had been their teacher; it was the Lord who had the relationship with the Father. All the miracles and blessings were coming from Jesus' intercessory prayers. However, all of that was about to change. As loving disciples, about to become teaching Apostles, they were going to have direct access to the Father in Heaven through the Holy Name of Jesus.

We too can have this direct access. Those of us who love and believe in Jesus Christ are members of what St. Peter calls a *"Royal Priesthood"* (1 Peter 2:9). Because our Risen Lord Jesus ascended to the Father in Heaven to rule at His right hand, we, His friends, can now go boldly before our Father's throne to ask for our needs to be met, in Jesus' name (Heb. 4). And, the Father who loves His children will give us mercy and grace according to our need.

No doubt there are things you'd like to change. We all have things we'd like to do better. But, what are your real needs? For what are you praying? Perhaps you have been hesitant to ask God because you feel unworthy. Remember, your Heavenly Father loves you and Jesus calls you friend, and His friends have benefits. When we take everything to the Father in prayer, this is life in Christ.

Notes

Discoveries from my path...

Day 3

"For I have come down from heaven, not to do my own will, but the will of him who sent me; and this is the will of him who sent me, that I should lose nothing of all that he has given me, but raise it up at the last day."

John 6:28-29

The Greatest Security

Too often people wonder if there is anything secure in our world. Everything seems unstable: jobs, families, even communities. We wonder if we've missed the will of God. Do you ever fear that you're not in God's will? When we're afraid, we often try to solve our insecurities by ourselves. We find ourselves working harder for bread that doesn't last, always thirsting for more and more of what never satisfies. Without Christ at the center of our lives nothing feels right. But, when we trust in Jesus, we are in the most secure place of all.

We don't have to wonder what the will of God is. Jesus tells us the Father's will is that everyone who sees Him will have eternal life (John 6:40). He assures us that we can trust Him. He won't lose a single one of us, if we continue to live for Him. The only question is, "Do we see Him for who He really is?"

Jesus is the Bread from Heaven. He is the one thing in this world that can meet every need and satisfy every desire providing our desires find their origins in Him. Too often we find the origin of our desires in the ways and wants of the world. Jesus wants to teach us to think and desire according to His kingdom principles, but first, we must open our eyes to see Him. We must see how much He loves us. We must trust He is working all things for our good even when it doesn't seem like it. When we trust in Jesus, the greatest security force in the world is holding us in the palm of His hand, and that's where we find life in Christ.

Notes

Discoveries from my path...

Day 4

John answered, "Master, we saw a man casting out demons in your name, and we forbade him, because he does not follow with us." But Jesus said to him, "Do not forbid him; for he that is not against you is for you."

Luke 9:49-50

God Loves Everyone

Perhaps the greatest tragedy of Christian history is the rise of sectarianism. It is apparently as old as the gospel itself. We can see its roots in the gospel account given by St. Luke. The disciples tried to prevent a man from casting out demons in Jesus' name because he was not one of them. It's a sign of our sinful nature that we so easily categorize people whom we perceive as different from us. However, there is only one humanity, and as the gospel teaches there is no need for categories; God loves everyone.

It is interesting to me that St. Luke tells the account of the man casting out demons in Jesus' name in the same narration as the disciples' debate as to their greatness. Jesus teaches them that rather than strive for greatness and recognition, they should strive for humility and child-like simplicity of faith. A child would not have cared if the exorcist were following them or not. The child would rather be excited to see someone else ministering in Jesus' name.

In our world today, division has become the common denominator of churches: catholic vs. protestant, white vs. black, conservative vs. liberal. In the kingdom of God, there may always be differences of opinion as to the interpretation of doctrine. God did not make us to think as robots programmed to the same opinions. However, God did make us to love and care for one another because we're all in this life together.

We need each other, and we need to learn how to serve each other, even those we perceive as different; they really aren't. And, as we serve them, we will grow to love them, for love conquers all; it is the language of the Kingdom of God. God loves everyone, and when we love like Him, we live life in Christ.

Notes

Discoveries from my path...

Day 5

It is written in the prophets, 'And they shall all be taught by God.' Everyone who has heard and learned from the Father comes to me. Not that anyone has seen the Father except him who is from God; he has seen the Father. Truly, truly, I say to you, he who believes has eternal life.

John 6:45-47

Hide and Seek

Interestingly, some people spend a lot of their life trying to figure out their purpose in the world while others seem to know it at an early age. The writer of Ecclesiastes said, *"...he has put eternity into man's mind, yet so that he cannot find out what God has done from the beginning to the end."* (Ecclesiastes 3:11). Without Jesus Christ, life really doesn't make sense; we live, we die. Some live lives of ease and wealth while others live in extreme hardship. But, with Christ in our life we begin to see God's plan. Yes, God does have a plan for each of our lives.

Jesus is not only the light of the world as we read in John 1, but he is also the bread of life, as we read in John 6. He is light for our path to show us the way, and he is bread to sustain us and nourish us along this journey we call life. In a way, life is like a game of Hide and Seek. We run away and hide and God seeks after us.

We run from God when we realize we've sinned. Like King David, our sin is ever before us. Yet God still seeks us. He loves us unconditionally, and no amount of sin can change that fact. What we need to do is stop running away. We need to stand still and be found.

There is a great theological truth revealed in today's verses. The truth is we don't find God. He finds us. The evangelical fervor of the last few centuries to spread the gospel has often focused the message on a call for the lost to find God. The message should rather be to encourage those who don't know Jesus to believe the one who already knows them, the one who found them, the one who has had them in his sights all along. Jesus makes it clear that no one can "find" Him, unless the Father first draws him or her. And, here is the really good news of the gospel; when we realize we've been found by God, we have eternal life.

In God's economy, no one is ever lost. God knows right where we are at all times. He is the Hound of Heaven, relentlessly seeking us in a cosmic game of Hide and Seek. Some are trying to hide from Him, but He won't stop seeking. In fact, He lets us know we've been found by calling out our name. Sadly, some choose not to answer His call.

If you're wondering just what your purpose is in this world, consider this; it is to be found by God. When you let Him find you, He can reveal His great plan for you; *"For I know the plans I have for you, says the LORD, plans for welfare and not for evil, to give you a future and a hope."* (Jeremiah 29:11). His plan is to give you life in Christ.

Notes

Discoveries from my path…

Day 6

I am the vine you are the branches. He who abides in me, and I in him, he it is that bears much fruit, for apart from me you can do nothing.

John 15:5

The Grapes of Grace

Have you ever heard the phrase, "Stay together, there's safety in numbers"? I remember walking through the streets of the old city of Jerusalem with a group of pilgrims. Our tour guide cautioned us not to separate from the group. On our own we could get lost, and while it wasn't an area of open rebellion and unrest, there were still those who could rob or harm us. Being together we were stronger, and we weren't easy prey for those who were bent on doing evil.

When we read Jesus' words about the vine and abiding in it so that we may be fruitful, many believers see Jesus is the vine, but fail to see that the vine is also a symbol for the church. In the Old Testament, the vine was always the symbol of the covenant people of God, Israel. And, in the New Testament, God still has a covenant people, the ecclesia (which means "called out group" in Greek), the church.

St. Paul tells us the Church (the people of God, the new Israel) is a great mystery that has now been revealed; it is the body of Jesus Christ, and we who believe are all members of His mystical body. For the body to be complete, all members are indispensable (1 Cor. 12:26, 27). If you are in Christ, you are a part of that body. The body of Christ needs you.

In recent centuries, there has been a great rise in an individualistic Christianity not known by the early church. In an effort to win the lost, the modern era has emphasized the individual decision to become a Christian (enter the covenant) over that of coming into the church, as the way of entering the covenant. As a result, a healthy understanding of the church has suffered.

While there is an individual aspect to understanding Christ as our Savior, we must remember that a thoroughly biblical theology of being saved is that of through God's covenant people, the vine. Whether it was by entering Noah's Ark, or by male circumcision (in which women were included as part of the family decision), or now, in the New Covenant, through baptism, there has always been a sacramental entrance rite into the covenant people of God (the Vine).

The vine is the only place for nourishment in this life. A branch separated from the vine cannot live for long; it will wither and die. Outside the vine, the world can be a dangerous place ruled by the principalities of darkness in the present age. We come to Jesus Christ the true Vine, through faith being drawn by His grace, and nourished by the sacraments of the church. In the sacrament of baptism, Jesus fully incorporates us into the vine. He feeds His branches with the sacramental food of the Eucharist, (the Lord's Supper). And, he supplies countless channels of grace through the Vine (Church) to His branches, so that they can bear much fruit.

What an amazing love, that Jesus would call us friends. That He would lay down His life for us so that we too may have His peace, His joy, His love, His life. On the vine (in the church), there is safety in numbers. On the vine, we find the grapes of God's grace, not the grapes of His wrath. *"If you abide in me, and my words abide in you, ask whatever you will, and it shall be done for you"* (John 15:7). This is life in the Church (Vine). This is life in Christ.

Notes

Discoveries from my path...

Day 7

But the Pharisees went out and took counsel against him, how to destroy him. Jesus, aware of this, withdrew from there. And many followed him, and he healed them all, and ordered them not to make him known. This was to fulfill what was spoken by the prophet Isaiah:

"Behold, my servant whom I have chosen, my beloved with whom my soul is well pleased. I will put my Spirit upon him, and he shall proclaim justice to the Gentiles.

Matthew 12:14-18

The Justice of Jesus

The ministry of Jesus was one of healing and hope. Wherever he went, he would take the time to heal those who sought him. Sometimes the healing was in public, as it was with the man with the withered hand in the temple. Other healings were often along the roadsides as crowds followed Jesus out of town; they couldn't let him get away without bringing their sick to him. Knowing the Pharisees were plotting to kill him, you would think he would have been in a hurry to get out of town, but not Jesus. Verse 17 tells us, *"and he healed them all"*. It is remarkable, that in the face of such injustice, even people trying to kill him, Jesus never waivers from his mission, a mission of hope, healing, and justice for all.

We can trust Jesus to never waiver from His mission. He is our king, our messiah, the redeemer of humanity, yet he is as St. Matthew quotes the prophet Isaiah, God's *chosen servant*. The life and ministry of Jesus brought hope and justice to a world without either. However, justice did not come in the usual way. There was no conquering or toppling of governments followed by a reordering of society to give equal rights to everyone. Instead, there was a suffering servant sent from God on a mission to bring healing and hope. Jesus did not cry out about his oppressors or proclaim a message of revolution in the streets. In fact, Isaiah tells us He wouldn't even break the rulers until He would bring justice in victory, a victory that would come only through his death. And, because Jesus conquered death by death, we now have the hope of true justice, of victory over death, through death.

The justice of Jesus is found only when we see that victory comes through death: death to self, death to this world, and death in this world. Once dead, then comes true life, a life of victory. No matter what injustice we face in this world, the suffering servant of God, Jesus Christ, is still on His mission until all enemies are put down, and the last enemy to be conquered will be death (1 Cor. 15:26).

Remember, because Jesus died we too must die, not just physically, but spiritually, as St. Paul says, we are to be *"crucified with Christ"* (Gal.2:20). Therein lies our real hope and justice, not in conquering this world and all our problems through worldly victories, but through the victory of Jesus' death on the cross, and through the hope of His resurrection from the dead. As St. Francis is said to have prayed, *"It is in pardoning that we are pardoned. It is in giving that we receive. And, it is in dying that we are born to eternal life."* Such is the justice of Jesus. Such is life in Christ.

Notes

Discoveries from my path...

Day 8

..., "Every man serves the good wine first; and when men have drunk freely, then the poor wine; but you have kept the good wine until now." This, the first of his signs, Jesus did at Cana in Galilee, and manifested his glory; and his disciples believed in him.

John 2:10-11

Saving the Best for Last

Is there anything more joyful than a wedding? I don't think so. Weddings are fun and exciting. Young couples have found the one to love for the rest of their lives. They've spent all their energy and resources for months, even years, getting ready for their big day, and what a big day it is. In fact, you could say it's miraculous. The book of Genesis tells us what weddings are all about; in it we read how a man leaves his father and mother and unites with his wife to become one flesh (Gen. 2:24; Mk 10:8).

The union of a man and woman in holy matrimony is indeed a miracle. They become as one in union with Christ. What a great mystery. God gave us this mystery precisely because it foreshadows all that our relationship is to be with God, in Jesus Christ through the power of the Holy Spirit. The wedding covenant is a metaphor for God which his people used throughout the Old and New Testaments. The Bride of Christ (the Church) is waiting the Bridegroom's (Jesus) coming to "marry" her, and take her to be with Him forever.

In the Wedding at Cana, Jesus performs His first miracle, as a foreshadowing of the greatest wedding that will ever be; the Marriage Supper of the Lamb, when Christ and His Bride (us) will be together forever. Jesus purposefully manifested his glory at such a beautiful and glorious occasion, thus beginning his public ministry as the Messiah. In His first miracle, turning water into wine, Jesus not only saved the wedding couple from great embarrassment, He brought them an even greater joy; the miraculous wine was the best of all.

Isn't it just like Jesus to save the best for last? One day, Jesus will come again. He will step back into this world, and usher in the greatest wedding of all time, when all the faithful who have gone before us, and the believers who remain, will suddenly be translated into the fullness of his glory, and so to be with Him forever.

Jesus always saves the best for last. You are his greatest work of creation. He made you to be with Him forever. Are you ready for your wedding day? A wedding takes a lot of preparation, but it is always worth it. Don't miss out on the best Jesus has for you. Come to the wedding, celebrate the feast. Jesus bids you, *"Arise, my love, my beautiful one, and come away"* (Song of Solomon 2:10) ... Come...to life in Christ.

Notes

Discoveries from my path...

Day 9

The official said to him, "Sir, come down before my child dies." Jesus said to him, "Go; your son will live." The man believed the word that Jesus spoke to him and went his way.

John 4:49-50

Miracles Happen When We Believe

What would our lives be like if we really believed the words Jesus speaks to us? Oh, I know we say we believe on some level, but real belief requires action on our part. Jesus speaks words of peace and joy into our lives. He tells us He will never leave us or forsake us. He even tells us that if we abide in Him and his word abides in us, that we can ask whatever we will in His name and it shall be done (John 15:7). Yet, most days many believers get up and go through their lives with very little peace and joy, and perhaps only hoping what they've asked of Jesus, He will do.

The official who begged Jesus to heal his son had two choices. He could continue to beg until Jesus would hopefully give in and come with him, or he could take Jesus at His word. He chose to act on his belief. It took real faith to leave the presence of this "so called" miracle worker, and go all the way home to a dying son. But scripture says he believed "the word" Jesus spoke to him.

Miracles happen when we believe Jesus and His word. For what miracle are you hoping Jesus will do? Have you come to Him, perhaps even begged Him? Perhaps you feel as if you're still begging Him? Prayer is sometimes about repeated begging, as in the parable of the woman who petitioned the unjust judge in Luke 18. Listen for His answer, *"Though I neither fear God nor regard man, yet because this widow bothers me, I will vindicate her, or she will wear me out by her continual coming."* (Luke 18:4, 5) You can trust in His answer, even if it's "No". Jesus not only knows what's best for you, He loves you more than anyone in the world. He is your Creator and Sustainer. He will only do, and allow what is best for you.

The most important thing in life is not that we "feel" all our prayers answered. We can rest in knowing He hears us and will answer in His good time. Rather, the most important thing is to believe. Miracles happen when we believe. To believe Jesus is life in Christ.

Notes

Discoveries from my path...

Day 10

Jesus said to him, "Rise, take up your pallet, and walk." And at once the man was healed, and he took up his pallet and walked. Now that day was the Sabbath.

John 5:8-9

Jesus Heals on the Sabbath

There are probably some in our world who are ill, and don't wish to get well. That may sound odd to you, but Jesus knows apathy is a real human emotion. Often those who suffer illness or poor conditions for many years often become used to the condition; they can't even imagine being whole or well. Jesus often asked those whom he healed if they wanted to be made well. Here we see a very important truth. Jesus will not heal us against our own will. In fact, healing, whether physiological, emotional, or in physical surroundings, can be said to occur when our will perfectly aligns with God's will. We must learn to see that healing isn't just the absence of disease or affliction, but the presence of wholeness in our spirit.

Jesus is always concerned for our spiritual lives. He knows what afflicts us. He desires for us to turn to him in times of distress or sickness, to look to him to make us whole. In the Bible, often times that wholeness was manifest in the cure of a disease or condition; this was to show Jesus' power over all things. Yet, each person whom He healed or raised from the dead went on to eventually become sick again, and die. We don't find healing in escaping death; rather we are born to our ultimate wholeness through death. The ultimate healing is to become one with Christ.

We must learn to see the mercy of God in all things. Even not being healed of a disease can be merciful. We don't know what the balance of our lives may hold, but Jesus does. Jesus, the Lord of life, knows what we need and will only do what is best for us. Jesus asks each of us the same question; *"Do you want to be healed?"* (John 5:6) When we truly desire the kind of wholeness that is only found in unity with Christ, then we are well on our way to healing. We are well on our way to life in Christ.

Notes

Discoveries from my path...

Day 11

And when they had eaten their fill, he told his disciples, "Gather up the fragments left over, that nothing may be lost." So they gathered them up and filled twelve baskets with fragments from the five barley loaves, left by those who had eaten.

John 6:12-13

Our Immeasurable God

One of the greatest worries of people in our world is how they will provide for themselves and their families. People go to great lengths to save money and invest wisely; trying to assure themselves they will not run out of money in retirement. Yet, in all this they often fail to consider that everything belongs to God and that He has promised to never let his righteous children be forsaken (Psalm 37:24-26). Sometimes, in the name of good stewardship, people forget that it's not just their hard work and wise ways with money which provide, but rather, it is the abundant grace of our immeasurable God.

In Scripture, bread is often a metaphor for the necessities of life. In John 6, Jesus goes on to tell the people that He is the bread of life. Jesus showed compassion for this crowd that followed him from miracle to miracle for days. It seems they had lost track of the time and found themselves in the Galilean wilderness, hungry and with little provisions for their extended time away. Being with Jesus was mesmerizing. They didn't want to leave and go home. The signs they saw, and the words they heard were amazing.

Jesus had compassion on the hungry crowds that day on the mountainside; five thousand people, and that didn't count the women and children. Can you imagine what was about to happen? About the time the people figured out they were hungry and didn't have enough food things would probably have gotten ugly. But, Jesus knew their needs. He took what little they had, two fish and five loaves of bread, and He fed every single person. And not only them, but 12 baskets full were leftover.

The twelve baskets represented the twelve tribes of Israel. Jesus showed them He was all they would ever need. Jesus knows what we need at every stage of our lives. What burdens are you carrying because you haven't yet realized that God has everything you need? His timing is always perfect. You can trust him to meet your need, even if you're in the desert. God delivered his children from Pharaoh, parted the Red Sea, fed them manna and quail in the wilderness, and even provided water from a rock. What do you need that He can't supply?

St. Paul reminds us in the Ephesians' letter, God is the God of immeasurably more (Eph. 3:20). There is no limit to his mercy, and no end to his provision. We can trust in his provision for us; this should give us confidence in the present, and hope for the future. This should bring us to faith in His providing grace for our lives. At the intersection of our need and God's supply, that's where we find life in Christ

Notes

Discoveries from my path...

Day 12

I myself did not know him; but he who sent me to baptize with water said to me, 'He on whom you see the Spirit descend and remain, this is he who baptizes with the Holy Spirit.' And I have seen and have borne witness that this is the Son of God."

John 1:33-34

Let the Blood Flow

Only one person can take away the sin in our lives, and that is Jesus. John calls him the "Lamb of God". He is the perfect, spotless Lamb slain for the forgiveness of sins. Yet, it remains for each person to enter into that forgiveness, to trust in Him for forgiveness. John's baptism (with water) was for repentance. By coming to the Jordon to be baptized, a person was saying, "I repent" They were saying, "I know I am a sinner, and I need to be forgiven." So, when the people came to be baptized, it was an act of faith believing forgiveness would somehow follow.

We know from John's words that Jesus did not need to be baptized for forgiveness because He was the spotless Lamb of God. Yet, in his baptism two very important things happen. One, Jesus sanctifies the act of water baptism for all to follow in it. Two, in His baptism, Jesus is revealed as the one who has the Holy Spirit, and He can give it to whomever he desires. John tells us that Jesus will offer a baptism of His own, a baptism with the Holy Spirit, through His blood.

Baptism is a cleansing act. To be baptized with the Holy Spirit is to be cleansed by the Spirit; just like salvation, which can only come by faith. When we are baptized with God's Holy Spirit, we are being washed in the blood of the Lamb, the soul-cleansing blood of the Lamb. This cleansing is the only thing that can wash away every stain of sin from our soul, and cleanse every part of our being to be sanctified, that is to be consecrated wholly unto God. Let the blood flow in our hearts, Lord Jesus!

To belong completely to God, to realize His desire to rule in our hearts, should be the goal of every believer. To live as such, we must be baptized with the Holy Spirit. In fact, if we are not baptized with the Holy Spirit, the gospels mention there will also be a time of baptism with fire, an unquenchable fire (Matt, 3; Luke 3,) that will separate believers from unbelievers.

Have you been baptized with the Holy Spirit? If you are not sure, you can be. Offer a prayer to Jesus now, asking Him to come into your heart and rule over every part of your life. Open every locked door and ask Him to cleanse every room of your heart. He is faithful, and He will do it (1 Thess. 5:24). Then, as you live each day, seek a closer walk with Him, guided by His Spirit in all things. To live in step with the Holy Spirit (Gal. 5:25) is to live life in Christ.

Notes

Discoveries from my path...

Day 13

The Spirit immediately drove him out into the wilderness. And he was in the wilderness forty days, tempted by Satan; and he was with the wild beasts; and the angels ministered to him.

Mark 1:13-14

Don't Fear the Desert

The wilderness can be a lonely, scary place. Few people went into the Palestinian wilderness alone. Usually the only persons you would see, if you saw any, were robbers. They would hide from the authorities in the desert wilderness, and rob those who came by. If one had to travel that way, it was important to travel in groups for safety. When Jesus went into the wilderness immediately after his baptism, he didn't go alone. The Holy Spirit went with Him. And, when you find yourself in the desert times of your life, you're not alone either. Don't fear the desert.

Jesus didn't fear the desert. In His humanity, Jesus knew it was there in the wilderness that the Father would come to him and confirm his calling. The road ahead of Him, the road to Calvary, was to be a long and lonely road. In the desert, Jesus would find the comfort of the Father through the ministry of the Holy Spirit. The strength He would find there to resist Satan was the strength he would need to go to the cross.

Are you feeling alone, and afraid? Can you hear Satan calling for you to give in to his worldly offers of fame, and fortune, if you'll just do things the way the rest of the world does? Remember, Jesus defeated the schemes of the devil with the promises of God's Word. Those promises are still true, and they're for you too. Promises like Psalm 91:

"He who dwells in the secret place of the Most High shall abide under the shadow of the Almighty.

I will say of the Lord, "He is my refuge and my fortress; My God, in Him I will trust."

Surely He shall deliver you from the snare of the fowler and from the perilous pestilence.

He shall cover you with His feathers, and under His wings you shall take refuge;"

Don't fear the desert. In the wilderness you will find God is your strength and shield, the One in whom you can always trust. In the desert you will find the power and the presence of the Holy Spirit to lead past sin and temptation. In the desert you will find life in Christ.

Notes

Discoveries from my path...

Day 14

And a leper came to him beseeching him, and kneeling said to him, "If you will, you can make me clean." Moved with pity, he stretched out his hand and touched him, and said to him, "I will; be clean." And immediately the leprosy left him, and he was made clean. And he sternly charged him, and sent him away at once, and said to him, "See that you say nothing to any one...

Mark 1:40-44

The Greatest Secret Ever Kept

They couldn't stay away from Jesus. It seems wherever he went the whole city came out to him. He couldn't even get alone to pray without the disciples finding him to let him know everyone was searching for Him. The scripture tells us people brought other people to see Jesus.

How different it is in today's world. If everyone still sought to be where Jesus is, our churches would be full. It's as if those of us who are in the church know where Jesus is, but we are keeping a great secret.

When the church is gathered in worship a mystery is manifested, it is the mystery of the body of Christ. Jesus is made present by the proclamation of His word, and the grace made present through His sacraments. The problem today is, too many people don't understand the mystery. St. Paul tells us, in Ephesians chapter three, the mystery has now been revealed in the church. He says we have "fellowship" in the mystery through the power of the Spirit.

Jesus Christ is present where two or three are gathered. Yet for his presence to be manifested we must realize He is here. Churches must rediscover the mystery of our faith and the grace that Christ wants to manifest to his people in and through the church. Where this is happening, people are seeking and finding. But, in too many places in our modern Western world all we see are half empty churches void of power.

Jesus always responds to humble faith like that of the leper. He broke all the rules when he came to Jesus and knelt at His feet. A leper was to keep a safe distance from everyone since his disease was highly contagious. Yet, in mercy Jesus reached out and touched him and made him clean. Though Jesus cautioned him not to tell anyone, the now healed man couldn't wait to tell everyone he knew about Jesus.

We too have all been healed of a great disease. The forgiveness of sin by Jesus Christ is the greatest miracle of all. Yet too many of us never tell a soul. Jesus asked those he healed not to tell because they couldn't really understand the miracle until after the cross. But, we live after the cross. We can understand that Christ died for us and that through His cross we are healed. How can we keep from singing that praise? How can we keep from telling our story? There is a world dying to hear about your faith. Will you tell it to them?

To tell your story of healing in Christ is to reveal the mystery to someone. To invite people to church is to invite them into the presence of Jesus, just like when people brought them to Peter's house. Will you go and tell? Will you go and bring? To do so is to believe in the mystery revealed in Christ. To do so is to live life in Christ.

Notes

Discoveries from my path...

Day 15

Which is easier, to say to the paralytic, 'Your sins are forgiven,' or to say, 'Rise, take up your pallet and walk'? But that you may know that the Son of man has authority on earth to forgive sins"—he said to the paralytic— "I say to you, rise, take up your pallet and go home."

Mark 2:9-11

A Pallet from a Friend

The man on the pallet had some great friends. Clearly they cared for him so much that nothing would stop them from bringing him to Jesus. Their faith was strong. They knew if they could just get their friend in front of Jesus, He would heal him. But Jesus' ministry was never meant to be about physical healing alone. Jesus came to bring the greatest healing of all, the healing of our souls from sin.

Often in life we fail to see our greatest need is not relief from sickness, pain, or disease. In fact, if Jesus were to heal us from disease or affliction, only to leave us in our sin, we would quickly be overcome by some other malady. Sin is at the heart of all our afflictions. Were it not for sin, we wouldn't have disease and death. There wouldn't be any pain or suffering. All of these are products of broken people who have broken other people, in a dark and broken world. But Jesus changed everything when he took our sin and brokenness upon Himself as he hung on the cross.

Jesus' death brought the greatest healing of all. He provided for our sin to be forgiven. He has transferred us from a world dominated by darkness to a kingdom of light (Col. 1:13). Those who sought healing for their friend on the pallet couldn't imagine a healing greater than their friend being made to walk again. Yet, by commanding the man to rise up and walk, Jesus showed them the priority is for forgiveness of sin. If he could perform the miracle of healing the man's legs, forgiving sin would then be a given in their minds since they perceived making the lame to walk as more difficult.

What great need do you have in your life? Could anything be too hard for Jesus? The Savior is looking into your soul and speaking words of love and healing, words of forgiveness. No matter what you've done, He knows about it, and He wants to forgive you. Please think of this devotional today as a pallet from a friend bringing you to Jesus. My desire is that you hear him say to you, "Your sins are forgiven". Can you hear Him? Now he commands you to rise up and walk. Walk in the light of his love and grace. Walk in the light of the life in Christ.

Notes

Discoveries from my path...

Day 16

And the scribes of the Pharisees, when they saw that he was eating with sinners and tax collectors, said to his disciples, "Why does he eat with tax collectors and sinners?" And when Jesus heard it, he said to them, "Those who are well have no need of a physician, but those who are sick; I came not to call the righteous, but sinners."

Mark 2:16-17

Friends in Lowly Places

I remember at the end of high school some of the most popular kids were voted "Most Likely to Succeed ..." There were lots of categories, things like business, sports, fame, riches etc. I don't know when that cultural trend started, and I don't know if they still do it in high schools today, but I'm always amazed at how wrong they are. Twenty and thirty years later, I meet people I was sure back then would be so successful, yet many of their lives have turned out radically different than anyone would have thought. Some have some pretty sad stories; others have reached places seemingly beyond hope. Yet, the message of the gospel is, no one is beyond hope. Jesus always finds friends in lowly places.

Levi, better known to us as Matthew, probably didn't set out in life to be a tax collector; one of the most hated of occupations. To collect taxes from his own people, and give them to the Romans was to put him in the status of traitor. What's worse, the tax collectors usually got rich skimming off the top by collecting more money than was actually owed, which made him a thief as well. Matthew's occupation left him with few friends in the mainstream of society. So, his life soon filled up his time with the other sinners and outcasts of his day. We can only imagine what some of their occupations were. Scripture tells us they were labeled sinners, as if to say those whom society deemed respectable were not.

When Levi met Jesus, everything changed. In fact, Jesus called Levi to be his disciple. And, Levi even went on to write the story of Jesus we know as the Gospel of Matthew. It was as if Jesus was determined not to build a respectable following. The Scribes and Pharisees were outraged. They wondered how a teacher of Israel could hang out with sinners and tax collectors, let alone make them his close companions. How? The answer is simple. Jesus always sees the heart of the individual, and he sees your heart too.

No matter what life has done to you, or where life has taken you that you never thought it would, Jesus can change your life just like he did Matthew's. Jesus is always calling for disciples. No one is beyond his reach. No heart is too cold or sinful for the Master's re- creating touch.

You may not have gotten off track as far as Matthew, but still, you may look at today and wonder, "How did I end up here?" It's not too late to change. It never is with Jesus. Today, if you hear his calling, as Matthew did, will you follow? The one promise I can make you is it will be worth it. Jesus won't let you down. St Paul says, *"Now is the day of salvation"* (2 Corinthians 6:2). Will you follow his voice? Will you step out in faith? To do so, is to find life in Christ.

Notes

Discoveries from my path...

Day 17

And he said to the man who had the withered hand, "Come here." And he said to them, "Is it lawful on the Sabbath to do good or to do harm, to save life or to kill?" But they were silent. And he looked around at them with anger, grieved at their hardness of heart, and said to the man, "Stretch out your hand." He stretched it out, and his hand was restored.

Mark 2:3-5

The Truth About Sabbath

You've probably heard the old saying, "There's no rest for the wicked." I've always wondered how that saying got started. Perhaps because wickedness is the work of the devil, and rest is the blessing of God. The whole idea of rest comes to us from the creation story in Genesis. We read that God "rested" from his work on the seventh day. In the Ten Commandments we also read God's command to us to "Remember the Sabbath to keep it holy". So, whatever we are supposed to learn about the Sabbath, the idea is that it is to be a holy time of rest. I really like that idea.

When I was in Israel, a few years ago, I arrived on Friday afternoon, just before Sabbath was to begin at sundown. I remember the cab driver telling me, "We've got to get you to your hotel before Shabbat (Hebrew word for Sabbath)! I can't work after sundown." As I relaxed at the hotel that evening, I observed a Jewish family having their evening meal together in the restaurant. It began with prayers and lighting a candle, and the whole evening seemed so relaxing to them. Then the next day, I noticed them relaxing all day reading, and visiting.

Jesus tells us in Mark 2:27, the Sabbath was made for man. God gave us a time to rest. We all need rest. There is a flow to our week of six other days to get our work done, but on the seventh, we are to rest. Why? Is it because it is sinful to work on our day of rest? No, it's because God knows we need the rest. We need time emotionally and physically for renewal.

When I was a boy, almost no one had to work on Sundays, which is the Christian observance of Sabbath in honor of the resurrection. The biblical Sabbath was sundown Friday to sundown Saturday). Almost all businesses were closed, a lot like I found it still is in Israel. However, if all we do with Sabbath is cease from work, we miss the point; Sabbath is to be holy. Our hearts and thoughts are to turn toward God, for worship, prayer, and renewal. We're also to enjoy the beauty of relationships God has given us in our family, friends, and creation. We don't observe Sabbath for the sake of keeping a rule; we observe it for the sake of entering into God's rest, which is filled with all good things. Sabbath is a time for all that is good in life.

Sabbath shouldn't be about keeping us from anything that is good. If we need to eat, then prepare food and eat. Jesus and his disciples went through the fields for grain because they needed to eat. If someone needs to be helped, by all means help him or her. Jesus healed the man with the withered hand because it was the right thing to do, Sabbath or not. Doing the right thing is always holy unto the Lord.

As you begin your weekend, will you have a Sabbath? I hope so. We all need one. God gave it to us as a gift for rest, and renewal. Keep the Sabbath in your heart, not just in what you do or don't do. The truth about Sabbath is that it's not a particular day of the week; it's a state of being. If you keep it in your heart, you will enter into God's rest. You will enter into life in Christ.

Notes

Discoveries from my path...

Day 18

So when the Samaritans came to him, they asked him to stay with them; and he stayed there two days. And many more believed because of his word. They said to the woman, "It is no longer because of your words that we believe, for we have heard for ourselves, and we know that this is indeed the Savior of the world."

John 4:40-42

Have You Heard for Yourself?

There are two ways we come to believe in something; because we are told of it, or because we have heard it for ourselves. As children we learn because our parents tell us, and we trust them to tell us the truth. However, as we grow our minds begin to search things out. We need to discover truth for ourselves. As concerns the truth of Jesus, do you believe in Him because you've heard it from others, or have you heard it for yourself? People who've heard for themselves have a testimony. Do you?

The woman at the well came back from meeting Jesus with a personal testimony. The Samaritan people believed the testimony of the woman. After all, he told her everything about herself; private things only she and God knew. At first her testimony was enough for the people to believe. But, eventually their faith grew. They went from second-hand knowledge that seemed believable, to first-hand knowledge they knew they believed. They went and met Jesus for themselves.

Most people's faith begins with second-hand knowledge about Jesus. Perhaps they hear it from a parent, a friend, or a preacher. Yet, for their faith to last, it must eventually become first-hand knowledge. Jesus cares for each of us, and for our faith. He comes to us revealing himself through others, scripture, and creation, until eventually, we have a personal encounter with Him. At this point we must do as the Samaritans did. We must choose to believe. We must believe for ourselves.

Personal, first-hand belief becomes our testimony. It is then that we can say along with the hymn writer of *Amazing Grace*, "I once was lost, but now I'm found, was blind, but now I see". How's your faith? Is it based on first-hand knowledge? Have you had a personal encounter with Jesus? He is still revealing himself to the world. That is why He sent the Holy Spirit, to convince the world of sin and of His truth (John 16:7-8).

What's your testimony? Take some time and think about it. There are some who are still operating on second hand knowledge. They haven't moved to a personal experience with Jesus. Often, people's second-hand faith, begins to fade, and sometimes they give up. They just decide it wasn't really authentic. I hope your faith is a first-hand one. But, if it's not there yet, pursue it for yourself. Seek a personal encounter with the Risen Lord. If you seek Him, you will find him. Deuteronomy 4:29 says, "*But if from there you seek the LORD your God, you will find him if you look for him with all your heart and with all your soul.*" To seek God with all your heart is to find life in Christ.

Notes

Discoveries from my path...

Day 19

Jesus withdrew with his disciples to the sea, and a great multitude from Galilee followed; also from Judea and Jerusalem and Idume'a and from beyond the Jordan and from about Tyre and Sidon a great multitude, hearing all that he did, came to him... And he appointed twelve, to be with him, and to be sent out to preach and have authority to cast out demons...

Mark 3:7-8, 14-15

Valleys of Decision

The prophet Joel spoke of great multitudes gathered in the Valley of Decision (Joel 3:14). In that chapter, his prophecy concerns many nations gathering to be judged by God. Interestingly, the multitudes who gather beside the Sea of Galilee to hear Jesus are not just Jews from Galilee, but also from Judea. Even the gentiles have come from beyond the Jordan and north from Tyre and Sidon. We see that from early in Jesus' ministry, He preached the gospel for everyone. Mountains surround the Sea, filling the valley that borders there with the actual seashore. There were so many people Jesus had to get into a boat to talk to the masses. There was no room left on shore making it a valley of decision. When Jesus teaches we must always decide if we will follow where He leads.

Perhaps there are many "valleys of decision" in our lives. Life is filled with mountain top experiences where we feel close to God, and then at other times, it's as if we feel we're in a valley far from God. It is usually in the valleys of life Jesus teaches us his greatest lessons. The question is will we listen and follow? Will we make a decision? Often we don't recognize Jesus is trying to teach us in the valley. Instead we raise doubts about God because he seems so far away. We don't feel the same presence the way we did on the mountaintop. Yet, God is always with us. He promised to never leave us or forsake us (Deuteronomy 31:6)

I wonder if Peter and the others who were called to follow Jesus, were wondering where this would lead. There they are in the middle of the crowd that day. They have been following along with the crowd, but that day Jesus called them to a special role in ministry. Mark 3:13 tells us Jesus walked up the mountain through the crowd and called the twelve whom he desired to make His Apostles. There he commissioned them to be sent out to preach and heal. They knew this was not going to be a short-term mission, and they were not going home to their families for a while. Jesus had kingdom work for them to do. A decision had to be made. Would they follow Jesus all the way?

Many times our valley decisions will be like that. Jesus may ask us to do something that requires more than we thought it would at the beginning. However, notice that Jesus didn't send the Apostles to work alone. He gave them His authority. And, he will not send you out from your valley alone either. Whatever Jesus calls you to go through He will go through it with you. Our God promises to go with us, to strengthen and uphold us with his righteous right hand (Isa. 41:10), to be with us even to very end of the age (Matt. 28:20). In your valleys of decision, always choose to follow Jesus. Then you will find His presence revealed within. Then you will find life in Christ.

Notes

Discoveries from my path…

Day 20

If a kingdom is divided against itself, that kingdom cannot stand. And if a house is divided against itself, that house will not be able to stand.

Mark 3:24-25

The Truth Hurts

In his U.S. Senate campaign in 1858, Abraham Lincoln gave a speech in which he quoted Jesus saying, "A house divided against itself cannot stand." (June 16, 1858 Illinois State Capital) Mr. Lincoln lost that race. However, his speech captured the truth of the times, as Americans were split over the issue of slavery. Two years later, Mr. Lincoln was elected President. In his 1858 Senate race, his campaign advisors wanted him to pull the quote from his speech. Mr. Lincoln wouldn't do it. He knew America needed the truth, and he also knew the truth hurts, but it's worth it.

Often we live lives divided against ourselves. We say we serve God and believe in him, and at the same time we live with one foot in the world trying to be all that the world wants us to be. We think if we will just cooperate with the world's way of doing things, we can be successful and still keep our place in the kingdom. But, Jesus demands we look at the world differently from the way it looks at itself. Christianity truly is counter-cultural. We can't live as the world does having a selfish, "What's in it for me" attitude, and expect God to bless our efforts. We must learn to live in harmony with others, seeking the good of others and stop putting our own interests ahead of others. Scripture teaches that God raises those who are humble, but He brings low those who try to promote themselves and their agendas.

Those who opposed Jesus felt they had to criticize His character; they said he was of the devil. Satan always promotes himself. But, Jesus always promotes others. He continually gave credit to the Father for all the miracles he performed. Jesus also promoted the sacredness of others by comparing those who followed him to being like his mother and brothers.

When you are tempted to compromise with the world, in order to get ahead, remember you can't serve two masters. Jesus has overcome the world. He has already tied up the strong man (Satan; Matt. 12:29) in our world and has the power to take back for God what the world seems to have won. Put your faith in Jesus. He is your healer, your sanctifier, and your truth. And remember, the truth may hurt, but it will always set you free (John 8:32), free to live life in Christ.

Notes

Discoveries from my path...

Day 21

And he said to them, "To you has been given the secret of the kingdom of God, but for those outside everything is in parables;"

Mark 4:11

Sowing Jesus

When I was young I used to think parables were a way of telling stories that would make the meaning clearer by using examples. Actually, it's just the opposite. The meaning of a parable isn't really clear at all. Yet, for those who seek out its meaning, there is great truth. Most of the time there are surface meanings that we assume are the main point, even though it misses the true and deeper meaning. The Parable of the Sower is perhaps one of Jesus' most famous parables. Many people think it's a story to help us understand there are four kinds of people who correspond to the four soil types; we need to be sure our lives are "good soil", that they are open to the Word of God, and will bear much fruit, but that's not all. There's so much more. There are actually five kinds of people in the story.

Of course we should want to lead lives that are made of the fourth soil type. You know the kind. They're people who are involved in church, read their Bibles daily, have deep prayer lives, and as a result the seed goes deep, and their lives yield much fruit doing lots of good works for others. But Jesus wants his disciples to go deeper than that. He doesn't want us to think in terms of what we get from the soil of our lives. He wants us to see that we, His disciples, are supposed to be the sower in the story. Many people assume, at a first glance, that the sower is Jesus sowing the gospel in our lives. But, Jesus tells us what the seed is, and it's not the gospel; it is the Word, and the Word (logos in Greek) is Jesus (John1:1).

The sower is the fifth kind of person in the story. Jesus expects his disciples to sow (share) Him in the world. Notice that the sower sows everywhere. The seed (Jesus, the word) comes into contact with everyone. Some people are ready for him, some people aren't. Nevertheless, the sower sows. The sower doesn't pick and choose where or upon whom to sow.

Have you identified yourself in this parable? We've probably all been the four different soils at one time or another. However, if we are intentional disciples, learning and growing daily in the Spirit of God, then as "fourth soil people" we will become sowers. When we receive the seed (Jesus the Word) into our soil, we have a responsibility to nurture and share it with others. To sow the word is to sow Jesus, and to sow Jesus is to live life in Christ.

Notes

Discoveries from my path...

Day 22

"And he said to them, "Is a lamp brought in to be put under a bushel, or under a bed, and not on a stand? For there is nothing hid, except to be made manifest; nor is anything secret, except to come to light."

Mark 4:21-22

The Light of the Kingdom

Anything that doesn't get used eventually wastes away. Metal turns to rust, water in a well stagnates, food, that is not eaten eventually spoils. All of us have cleaned out our refrigerators. So it is with our lives, if we don't clean them properly. Jesus says that we (believers in Christ) are the light of world. We are like lamps that need to stand out in the open to give light to those in darkness. If we hide our light under a bushel, we will soon find ourselves in the darkness as well. When we give away the light God has given us, He gives us even more. But, if we don't use that light, it too may one day fade from our lives

Jesus Christ is the source of all light. He is the uncreated light that existed before the formation of the world. Jesus' teachings on the kingdom of God shed light on our lives in relationship to the church and the world around us. He compares the kingdom to a mustard seed. It is only when a seed dies in the ground that it produces life. In dying for us Jesus made real life possible, even eternal life. When you consider your life today, rather than consider the many problems and issues you are facing consider the kingdom of God, and how it overshadows everything around us. The answers you seek will always be found within the kingdom. The mustard tree is a beautiful metaphor for the kingdom. It began as a tiny seed and over time became a mighty tree, so too the Kingdom of God.

God gave birth to the church here on earth by sending the Holy Spirit. Over the centuries, through the dying service of her apostles and martyrs, and the faithfulness of the Holy Spirit to nurture and inhabit her many branches, the church of God is now the greatest life force in the world. She is spreading the good news to all nations and peoples. The answers to the problems that infect and affect her myriads of branches (you and me) are always found through the life giving force of the Holy Spirit within the kingdom (church).

In the fifth century, Bishop Peter Chrysologus, described the kingdom like this:

"Sown like a mustard seed in the garden of the virgin's womb, he grew up into the tree of the cross whose branches stretch forth across the world. Crushed in the mortar of the passion, its fruit has produced seasoning enough for every living creature with which it comes in contact. As long as a mustard seed remains intact, its properties lie dormant; but when it is crushed they are exceedingly evident. So it is with Christ; he chose to have his body crushed, because he would not have his power concealed.... Christ became all things in order to restore all of us in him."

When you think about your problems today, would you

consider them in the context of His kingdom? Would you consider that through dying Jesus birthed the kingdom? And, in his passion he provided the cure for all that ails us. We must use the light He has given us to look into the true light that is in Him. There we will find our answers. There we will find the healing Isaiah promised would come through his stripes (Isa. 53:5). There we will find the true light. There we will find life in Christ.

Notes

Discoveries from my path...

Day 23

He said to them, "Why are you afraid? Have you no faith?" And they were filled with awe, and said to one another, "Who then is this, that even wind and sea obey him?"

Mark 4:40-41

Jesus Is in the Boat

Fear is universal. All people feel it at one time or another. What is fear? The dictionary says it's a "distressing emotion aroused by impending danger, whether real or imagined". However, when as believers in Christ we think about all God has promised, I think a different definition is needed. Fear is, believing a lie from the devil. When we're afraid, it seems we act as though we don't know who Jesus is.

The disciples did not really know who Jesus was, that he could command the sea and the wind; they were afraid even though Jesus was in the boat with them. Did they think Jesus would really let them perish in the storm? Well, they probably weren't really thinking at all. That's what we do when we allow fear to grip us. God has promised to never leave us or forsake us (Deuteronomy 31:6). In fact, nothing can happen to us that He doesn't know about (Lamentations 3:37).

What are you afraid of? Many people live in fear. They fear they will get a disease, fear not having the finances to pay their obligations or to retire, fear losing their job, fear dying. The list goes on and on. Yet, how is this trusting in God? Psalm 27 states the truth that *"The Lord is the strength of my life,"* Then, the psalmist asks the question, *"Of whom shall I fear?"*

My good friend, Jaco Booyens, a former professional athlete, motivational speaker, and the founder of After Eden Pictures, a Christian Film Company, has a powerful message on fear. Jaco says, "Fear is a lie from the devil", and he's right. Satan wants to rob God's people of their peace; he wants to plant doubts in your mind about God's promises, just as he did with Eve in the Garden. He is the father of lies. So why do we listen to such lies? Why do we fear? It seems we've forgotten that Jesus is in the boat with us. Believers don't go anywhere without the indwelling Spirit of God.

Today, consider your fears in this life, and call them out. Stand on the promise that Christ is with you and in you. God has always been with his people. As the children of Israel were about to enter the Promised Land, they were tempted to fear the inhabitants of it. In Deut. 31:8, Moses said to Joshua, *"The LORD is the one who goes ahead of you; He will be with you. He will not fail you or forsake you. Do not fear or be dismayed."*

In scripture, over and over we hear the command, "be not afraid". In fact, it is a direct command from Jesus. He said, *"Do not be afraid"* (Matthew 14:27). Shouldn't we trust the One who made us, the One who died to save us? There is no boat you can get into today and no storm that can arise in your life that Jesus doesn't already know about. So, when you are tempted to fear, take Jesus' words to the wind and waves and hear Him whisper them into your life... *"Peace, be still"* (Mark 4:39). To live in peace, is to live life in Christ.

Notes

Discoveries from my path...

Day 24

And they came to Jesus, and saw the demoniac sitting there, clothed and in his right mind, the man who had had the legion; and they were afraid.

Mark 5:15

Love Conquers All

Demon possession is an often-misunderstood danger in our spiritual world today. Some Christians see demons in all kinds of behavior and things. They see them as just waiting to devour people's spirits. However, we must make a very important distinction here: while we can't deny the existence of demons in the world, we must not live in fear of them either. Demons cannot possess a Christian believer.

The Light of the world (Jesus) inhabits believers, and John makes it clear in his first epistle that darkness and light cannot coexist in the same place (1 John 1:5). Therefore, as inhabitants of the Light, we fear not the powers of darkness. Love conquers all.

Often we fear things in this world. Yet, fear does not belong in the life of the Christian. The people who came out to witness whether the demon- possessed man was healed were afraid of

Jesus. In the face of the greatest love in the world, they found fear. Why? They had no experience with such love.

Many of the town's people were probably gentiles since the Decapolis was a Greek area east of Galilee. They were swine herders, which were forbidden in a Jewish community. As gentiles they were pagans if they were religious at all. Pagan religions believed in evil gods and clearly they thought the young man had an evil spirit. They couldn't imagine a force with such love as Jesus, great enough to cast out the demon.

Scripture teaches us that perfect love casts out all fear (1 John 4:8). Jesus' love is perfect. There is nothing in this world that should give us fear if we are trusting in Jesus for our salvation. The testimony of a believer is a powerful witness against the darkness.

The people of the community begged Jesus to leave them; they wanted to go back to the dysfunctional lives they knew. But the power of witness eventually won them over. Jesus would not let the healed man go with him. He knew the man's testimony would be a great witness for the love of the true God.

We too must learn to trust God's love to conquer all our fears. Nothing can harm those who are in Christ. Disease, war, and hatred may take our lives, but it cannot take our souls. We are safe in the arms of a loving God. We must learn to sing with the psalmist:

"Bless the LORD, O my soul, and forget none of His benefits; Who pardons all your iniquities, who heals all your diseases; Who redeems your life from the pit, who crowns you with loving-kindness and compassion" (Ps 103:2-4)

Whatever your fears today, would you give them to the Lord

of Life? Would you sing out to Him a song of praise, blessing, and honor, for He has redeemed you and made you His own? You are the joy of His life. To sing as His child is to live, life in Christ.

Notes

Discoveries from my path...

Day 25

When Jesus saw him and knew that he had been lying there a long time, he said to him, "Do you want to be healed?"

John 5:6

People Matter Most

God's mercy is greater than all our excuses. The man Jesus healed by the pool had been ill for thirty-eight years. That's a long time. In fact, Jesus knew he'd been coming to the pool every year in hopes of being healed. The pool had an amazing effect on the lame. They believed an angel would come into the waters and stir them up, and the first one in would be healed.

It does seem hard to imagine that after so many years the man couldn't have made it into the waters first. After all, he made it to the pool every day. Couldn't he make it in the water just once? Perhaps he had given up hope of healing. Perhaps he even wondered if God cared. But, all that changed the day he met Jesus. Looking into Jesus' eyes of mercy, he found the strength to obey, to rise up and walk.

The Jews thought that illness and disease was a consequence

of sin in one's life. Of course, understanding we live in a fallen world we realize that isn't necessarily so. Bad things do happen to good people through no fault of their own. However, maybe this man had lived a life of sin. Perhaps his illness was a consequence of such a life. We can't say for sure, but it does show the love of God for us even in our sinful estate. Jesus admonished the man to go and sin no more, lest something worse happen to him.

Jesus' mercy is available to everyone. We have all sinned, and in Jesus' great mercy He brings healing grace to us in our times of greatest need. Nothing can stop the mercy of God. Not the day of the week or the time of year. His mercy is available 24/7 because people matter most. What really matters to God is that we know how much he loves us.

God loves you more than anything in creation. Jesus and the Father are still working; working to show you how important you are. Will you respond to Jesus' offer of mercy? It doesn't matter what you've done, He still wants to forgive you, to show you how much you are loved. Knowing all this, will you rise up and walk? Will you walk in the light of His healing and restoration? To walk as such is to live, life in Christ.

Notes

Discoveries from my path...

Day 26

While he was still speaking, there came from the ruler's house some who said, "Your daughter is dead. Why trouble the Teacher any further?"

Mark 5:35

Never Too Busy

Aren't you glad Jesus is never too busy for one more request? Everywhere Jesus went crowds pressed in around him. In today's gospel Jesus is once again by the seashore, a place where He loved to teach the people. It was always Jesus' mode of operation to teach wherever He went. However, this day, there wasn't time to teach. Immediately he was asked to go and heal Jairus' daughter. Even as he left, the crowds followed, and in the middle of the crowd came a woman desperate to be healed. Nothing could keep her from Jesus.

She had been sick for twelve years. And, she had spent all of her savings on medical treatments. Probably sounds familiar to many reading this today. Like the woman with the issue of blood, we too must not let anything keep us from Jesus. One might think after twelve years and spending all her money she would have lost faith in ever being healed. But, her faith told her this time it would different. Even though all other attempts had failed, this time she was able to go straight to the Great Physician. Her faith told her it didn't matter if Jesus was swamped with other needs all around him. If she could just touch the hem of his garment, she knew he could heal her. What great faith!

As children of God, experiencing new life in Jesus, we don't have to hope to touch the hem of his garment. We don't have to hope He isn't too busy for our needs. The writer of Hebrews reminds us that because of Jesus, who is our great High Priest, we can go boldly into the presence of God. We can go straight to the, *"throne of grace"* to find mercy for all our needs (Heb. 4:16).

What needs have you forsaken because you've carried them so long you thought God forgot about you? What pain are you secretly carrying, stuffing it way down deep within, and trying to forget about it? Jesus is waiting for you at the throne of grace. The old hymn is true: *"Oh what needs we often forfeit. Oh what needless pain we bear. All because we do not carry everything to God in prayer."* (What A Friend We Have In Jesus, Joseph Scriven).

Jesus has healing for you today. Perhaps it's physical healing. Or, perhaps it's spiritual healing to give you grace to help you carry your burden a while longer. When we come to Christ, we give up all our own desires in exchange for His. We pray, "Not my will, but Thy will be done". Gene Williams, a former pastor of mine used to say, *"Jesus is too good to do wrong, and too wise to make a mistake"*. He's never too busy for you. You can trust Him. To trust in Jesus is to live life in Christ.

Notes

Discoveries from my path...

Day 27

And Jesus said to them, "A prophet is not without honor, except in his own country, and among his own kin, and in his own house."

Mark 6:4

Right in A Wrong World

Being a Christian isn't always easy. If we live our faith seriously, we will be at odds with the values of the world around us. The world teaches us to be first. The gospel tells us to be last. The world says we must stand up for ourselves. The gospel says to turn the other cheek. It's not easy not to speak up for what we know is right when we are being told we're wrong. When we do, it usually ends in an argument, and few people are ever won to the kingdom by arguing. However, walking away without defending ourselves when we know we're right, can speak louder than words. It's hard being right, in a wrong world, but it can be done.

The gospel is truth. When lived out before the world, such truth will draw those whom God knows are willing to hear (John 12:32). But, there will always be some who don't hear. Jesus told his disciples to walk away and to shake the dust of the town from their feet as they left. He knew what it felt like to be rejected. As Jesus brought the good news to his hometown of Nazareth, He watched people he had known all his life reject him. That hurts. He showed them the love of God himself, yet they could not see who He was.

There will be times in your life when it seems everyone is against you. You're trying to live righteously, but they don't appreciate your morals or ideals. It feels wrong. In the face of such love, shouldn't people hear and be changed? Shouldn't they turn to Jesus and repent? Instead they persecute you. Jesus says you're in good company. They also persecuted the prophets who were before you (Matt. 6:10-12). When this happens, Jesus says you are blessed! He also promises a crown of victory to those who overcome (Rev. 2:10).

We are called to live right, in a world that lives wrong. We are called to give, in a world that steals. We are called to love, in a world that hates. But take heart Jesus has overcome the world, and so will you, if you persevere. Jesus says, *"Blessed are you when people insult you and persecute you, and falsely say all kinds of evil against you because of Me. "Rejoice and be glad, for your reward in heaven is great..."* (Matthew 5:11). Such is the way, of those who follow Jesus. Such is the way, of life in Christ.

Notes

Discoveries from my path...

Day 28

And the king was exceedingly sorry; but because of his oaths and his guests he did not want to break his word to her.

Mark 6:26

Making Right Choices

Herod had a history of making bad decisions. He rose to power through a life of duplicity, making friends with the Romans so that he could rule over his own people. He wasn't even a valid king, having no lineage that would qualify him as the ruler of Israel. Once in power, he continued to make bad choices. His lifestyle was sinful and depraved, seeking only his own pleasure. Yet even as sinful as Herod was, the gospel came to him offering him a choice. The gospel reaches to everyone.

John the Baptist pointed Herod to the truth of Jesus. Scripture tells us in Mark 6:19-20, Herod realized John was a holy man. In the face of holiness, he feared Him, even protected Him. However, in the end, his sin won. His arrogance and pride made promises he didn't want to keep, but did. Showing he ultimately had no morality, he chose what he knew to be wrong, and put a holy man to death. Clearly, Herod cared nothing for his subjects.

The world tries to lure us into sin one small choice at a time. Herod was power hungry, but I doubt in the beginning of his career he ever thought he would put the innocent Son of God to death. Sin will always take us farther than we ever thought it would in the beginning. Sin masquerades as fun for a while, only to turn on us in the end leaving us alone and empty.

Whatever your temptations are, know that you don't have to give in to them. St. Paul tells us, *"No temptation has overtaken you that is not common to man. God is faithful, and he will not let you be tempted beyond your strength, but with the temptation will also provide the way of escape, that you may be able to endure it."* (1 Cor. 10:13).

The Spirit is always convicting us with knowledge of right and wrong, even as He did Herod. Yet, it remains for us to choose. And, the more we allow temptation into our lives, the harder it is to choose right. The harder it is to live, life in Christ.

Notes

Discoveries from my path…

Day 29

The apostles returned to Jesus, and told him all that they had done and taught. And he said to them, "Come away by yourselves to a lonely place, and rest a while."

Mark 6:30-31

Bringing Balance to Life

Life can be noisy. If we're not careful, we will find ourselves so busy we can't hear anything but the noise around us. Sometimes, I feel like I can't even hear myself think. That's when I realize I need to get away for some quiet time. Everyone does. Parents need a break from their kids. Men and women need time away from their jobs, and even Jesus needed a break from the crowds. The ministry had become overwhelming. Jesus taught his disciples they needed to have some quiet time to restore balance to all things.

Too much of anything can be a bad thing. Well, okay, I know some of you are thinking of your favorite thing - chocolate or coffee perhaps. But really, if you have too much it's going to have an adverse effect. Sadly, for Jesus and his disciples that day, it didn't get better. No sooner had they gotten away across the lake when the crowds followed them. Mark 6 tells us Jesus saw them as sheep without a shepherd, so He had mercy on them. He continued to teach them, and when the hour grew late, and the disciples reminded Him they were tired and hungry, He stopped to feed them.

Jesus fed over 5,000 people miraculously with only two fish and five loaves of bread. Only God could do that! And in the midst of feeding all the people, I'm sure once the disciples sat down to eat they felt refreshed. I know the text doesn't say that, but think about it. When Jesus feeds us, he feeds us the bread of life, the bread that truly satisfies (John 6:55).

Let me ask you a question. How long has it been since you really got away from it all? That long, huh? Jesus wants to restore balance to your life. Only He can. All other attempts to bring balance to life eventually leave us wanting.

Do you have a regular routine of getting away to a quiet place to spend time with Jesus? That's where the disciples were headed. Jesus wasn't sending them away by themselves when they first crossed the lake. They were headed to a lonely place with Jesus. Only when night came did they get away without Him. Then he went away to commune with His Father in prayer.

Won't you take some time, maybe even today, and get away? Plan some down time, not to socialize with a friend at lunch or to play a game, but to spend time with the Lover of your soul; the One who can refresh your very being. To do so is to bring balance to your life. To do so is to live, life in Christ.

Notes

Discoveries from my path...

Day 30

And he got into the boat with them and the wind ceased. And they were utterly astounded, for they did not understand about the loaves, but their hearts were hardened.

Mark 6:51-52

Hindsight Is Always 20/20

Fear is an often-repeated theme in scripture. It seems as though the disciples shouldn't have feared so much seeing Jesus walk on water, after being with Him and seeing all the miracles He performed. Clearly he was the Son of God. Yet, they couldn't grasp the fullness of what that meant. But, we can't be too hard on them. It wouldn't be till after the cross, resurrection, and Pentecost they would be able to understand who Jesus really was. You and I are living after the gift of Pentecost, and sometimes we still don't seem to get all of who Jesus really is. But after things calm down, then we can see the true meaning of events. Hindsight is always 20/20.

After a busy few days of constant crowds they were in serious need of rest. And then it was a tough night on the sea. They weren't getting any rest fighting the waves. When they saw someone walking on the water, they were immediately afraid.

That was a pretty strange thing. Nobody can walk on water. In ancient times, the sea was a dangerous place of great mystery, full of giant creatures. The pagan world had gods of the sea, and men believed that to rule the waters was to rule the world. When Jesus walked on the water, he was showing the disciples He was greater than any ruler of men, or any so called god of the sea. But all they saw was a ghost. They were afraid.

What things do you fear in this world? While fear is a common human emotion, even instinct in danger, we really shouldn't fear if we are in Christ. The power of the resurrection is the power that indwells the Spirit-filled Christian. St. Paul prays that he may, *"know the power of His resurrection"*, and then in the same thought acknowledges that it comes with the *"fellowship of His suffering"* (Phil. 3:10). Often our fears are tied to our not wanting to suffer.

While we should not wish to suffer, we should accept suffering as a part of Christian life. Jesus told his disciples they would suffer, but he also told them not to fear. He said, "*I have told you all this so that you may have peace in me. Here on earth you will have many trials and sorrows. But take heart, because I have overcome the world."* (John 16:33)

Look at your fears. What are they? Ask yourself, "Why am I afraid?" Then claim the power of the resurrection to conquer your fears. Look back on all you've been through. You've suffered before. You've been afraid before. But, you made it through. With Jesus, we will always make it through. With Jesus we can trust the future. It doesn't matter what will happen. He will be with us no matter what we may encounter. *"If Christ is for us, who could be against us?"* (Rom. 8:31) Nothing can separate us from the love of Jesus. This is what it means to live, life in Christ.

Notes

Discoveries from my path...

Day 31

"Truly, truly, I say to you, he who believes in me will also do the works that I do; and greater works than these will he do, because I go to the Father.

John14:12

Power to Live

In the days preceding His crucifixion, Jesus knew His disciples were troubled by His talk of dying. He tried to comfort them with words about their future home with the Father and with Him, a home to which He would one-day return and take them. However, to return He had to go.

They couldn't understand His talk of going away. They wanted to always be with Jesus. Philip speaks for all of us when asks the Lord to show them the Father (Vs. 8). Jesus kept talking about going to the Father, and how wonderful the Father's house was. It was frustrating them to not be able to just see and know the Father as they could see and know Jesus. Sensing their frustration, Jesus takes the opportunity to share two most important things they would not really understand until they received the gift of the Holy Spirit. These two things would shape their entire ministry.

What they were learning is there is no shortcut to powerful living. First, He told them in seeing Him, they have seen the Father. Jesus is God. The Father is in Him and He is in the Father. Jesus was teaching them about the Trinity, though they would only understand later. The Father and the Son are different persons but one in being (John 14:11). The writer of Hebrews says it so well. Describing Jesus, he says, *"He is the radiance of the glory of God and the exact imprint of his nature, and he upholds the universe by the word of his power..."* (Hebrews 1:3a) The last statement about Jesus upholding the universe by His power is the key to the second point Jesus was teaching the disciples.

Second, Jesus tells them that as great as the works they have seen Him do have been, they will do even greater works. How could this be? They were only men, but He is God. We need to understand this point. In it lies the power to living the victorious life. When we believe in Jesus and live in the power of His Spirit, nothing is impossible. We have the power to ask in Jesus' name for anything that is in accordance with the Father's will, and Jesus says it will be done. Wow!

When we reach a place of understanding this, it changes the world around us. We become Jesus' ambassadors, acting on His behalf, and in His power. That is why in the early church the apostles, healed the sick, and even raised the dead. This is the power Jesus wants for the church in our world in every generation. The problem is, too often we don't believe as they believed. Too often, we try and take shortcuts to a deeper relationship.

To believe and act in the power of Jesus' name is to be His witnesses. The disciples spent three years walking with and learning from Jesus. Yet, they were only ready to live in the power of His name after they fully surrendered and received the gift of His Spirit. Only then did they really know how to ask in Jesus' name. You and I are on a journey of discipleship, growing ever closer to our Father through Jesus. The more time we spend with the Father, the more He reveals His will to us. And, when we know His will we know how to live as witnesses to the incredible power of Jesus' name.

Instead of living in despair at how powerless the church seems to be in the world, we need to be intentionally hungering for a deeper relationship with the Father. The church is only as powerful as her witnesses. As Jesus draws us deeper, He works His will into our lives, and we begin to see His will being shaped in our lives and in our world. Living deeply in the Spirit of Christ is our calling. There are no shortcuts to deep living. Living each day in the power of His Spirit is living life IN Christ.

Notes

Discoveries from my path...

About the Author

Brad Riley is an ordained minister in the Church of the Nazarene, with a Catholic background in his youth. His heritage has given him an appreciation for the historic faith of the one, true, catholic, and apostolic Church. As a minister he loves all branches of Christianity. He believes everyone is on a journey to know truth, and Jesus Christ is that Truth. A good friend has coined a new phrase for him... *"Orthocathorene"*; part Orthodox, part Catholic, and part Nazarene. He takes that as a high compliment.

Brad's work in the community often opens up opportunities to minister in ecumenical settings where he meets with families from various or no theological backgrounds. What really matters to those families is not his denomination or creed, but that he shares the love of Jesus with them in some of their most difficult times.

Brad and his wife Rhonda have served churches in San

Antonio, Texas and Wichita, Kansas. They have been married for 30 years and have two children. They reside in Wichita, Kansas, where he currently serves as Associate and Teaching Pastor of the First Church of the Nazarene. He is also the founder of The Merciful Servants of Christ, a discipleship order for spiritual formation, and The Ecumenical Christian Prayer Group. He also travels to speak in churches and organizations inspiring them to grow deeper as intentional disciples of Jesus Christ.

Additional Resources

Learn more about Pastor Brad's ministry at

www.bradrileyministries.com

Read more from Pastor Brad on his devotional blog

www.pastorbradmsc.com

Subscribe to Pastor Brad's email devotions at

http://www.bradrileyministries.com/subscribe-blog

Learn more about the Merciful Servants of Christ at
http://www.bradrileyministries.com/msc

Learn more about the Ecumenical Christian Prayer Group at
https://www.facebook.com/EcumenicalChristianPrayerGroup/

Follow Pastor Brad on Twitter @pastorbradmsc

https://twitter.com/pastorbradmsc